What's Going on When It's

by Noah Leatherland

Minneapolis, Minnesota

Credits
Images are courtesy of Shutterstock.com. With thanks to Getty Images, Thinkstock Photo, and iStockphoto. Cover – MeSamong, LAUDiseno, AlexanderTrou, koblizeek. Texture throughout – MeSamong. 4–5 – Pakhnyushchy, KAMONRAT, Studio_G. 6–7 – Kongpraphat, Andrei Stepanov, muratart. 8–9 – ch123, nadia_if, Anditya Creative. 10–11 – schankz, Frau aus UA, Aligator Pro, Receh Lancar Jaya. 12–13 – Aleksei Ignatov, Marinka Buronka. 14–15 – E Forafontova, BlueRingMedia. 16–17 – Just dance, EugeneEdge. 18–19 – movchanzemtsova, LightField Studios. 20–21 – CandyBox Images, Scherbinator, BRO.vector. 22–23 – Maria Sbytova, inspiring.team, YanLev Alexey.

Bearport Publishing Company Product Development Team
Publisher: Jen Jenson; Director of Product Development: Spencer Brinker; Managing Editor: Allison Juda; Editor: Cole Nelson; Associate Editor: Naomi Reich; Associate Editor: Tiana Tran; Art Director: Colin O'Dea; Designer: Kim Jones; Designer: Kayla Eggert; Product Development Specialist: Owen Hamlin

Library of Congress Cataloging-in-Publication Data is available at www.loc.gov or upon request from the publisher.

ISBN: 979-8-89232-870-8 (hardcover)
ISBN: 979-8-89232-956-9 (paperback)
ISBN: 979-8-89232-900-2 (ebook)

For more information, write to Bearport Publishing, 5357 Penn Avenue South, Minneapolis, MN 55419.

CONTENTS

WHAT IS WEATHER?

Weather is what it is like outside. The weather is always changing.

Many things can affect the weather. Rain storms can make weather wet. Winter can bring snow and ice.

WHAT'S GOING ON WHEN IT GETS COLD?

TEMPERATURE

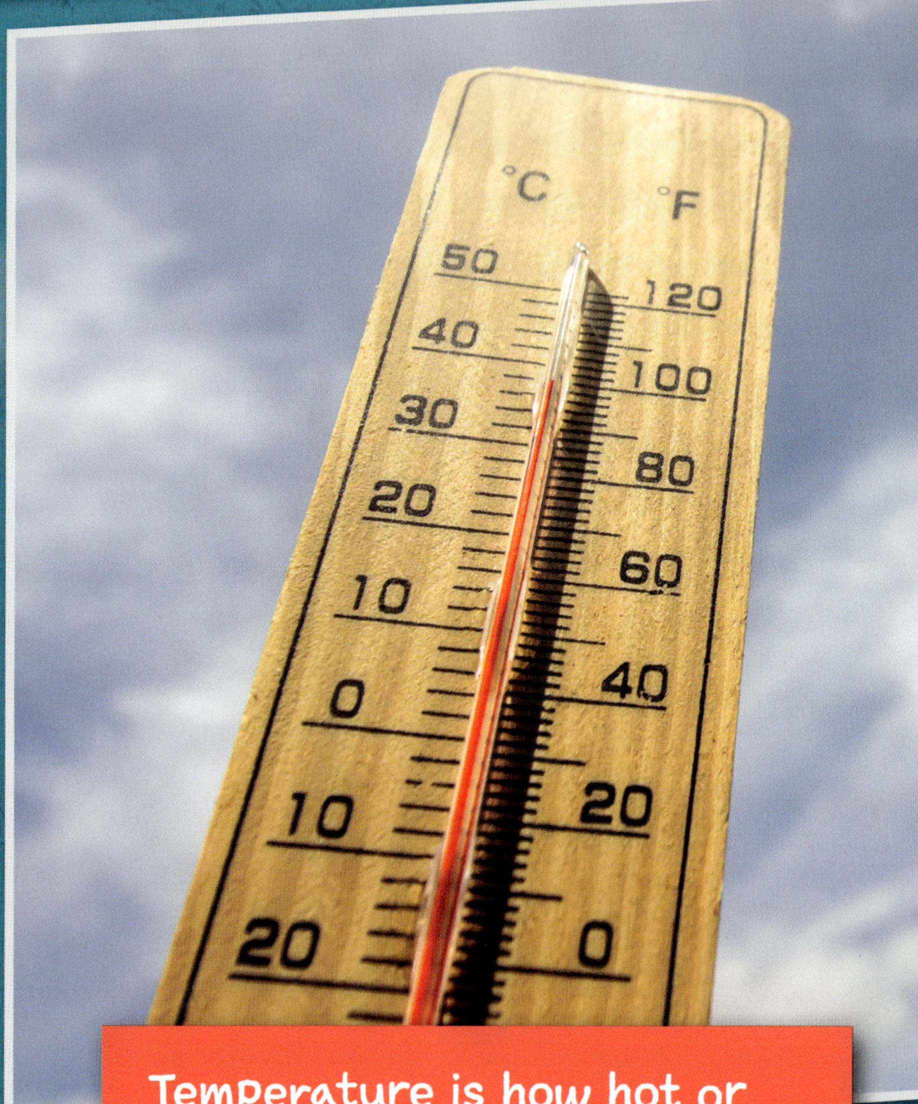

Temperature is how hot or cold something is. It is one way to measure the weather.

Some places are hot or cold all year. Others change temperatures each season.

COLD WINTERS

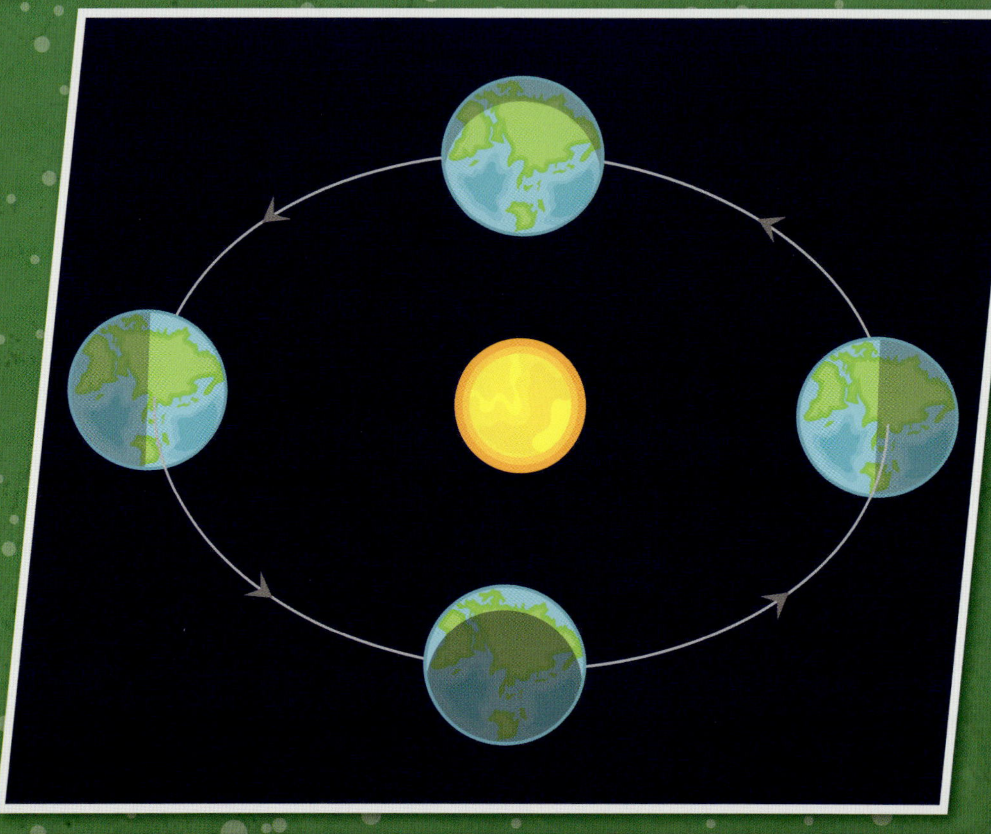

Seasons happen because Earth is **tilted** as it goes around the sun. This means Earth's top and bottom halves do not get the same amount of sunshine.

This tilt causes the seasons to change. It is winter where Earth is tilted away from the sun.

ICE

Water freezes when the temperature gets very cold. It turns into ice.

Ice forms on the ground when it is cold. Be careful around ice. It is very slippery!

SNOW

Snow is made up of tiny ice **crystals.** These crystals stick together in cold clouds to make snowflakes.

Sometimes, snowflakes are very small. But often small flakes join together. They make bigger snowflakes as they fall.

HAIL

Hail is made of water that freezes in thunderclouds. As the hail gets bigger and heavier, it starts to fall.

Pieces of hail are called hailstones. Most hailstones are tiny. But some can be bigger than golf balls!

SHIVERING

Cold weather can make your body cold, too. You might start to **shiver**.

Your **muscles** tighten and relax very quickly when you shiver. This is one way your body can warm up.

HYPOTHERMIA

Getting too cold can be dangerous. **Hypothermia** happens when your body cannot warm up when it is cold.

Mittens and scarves help you stay warm. Always cover up in warm clothes before going out in the cold.

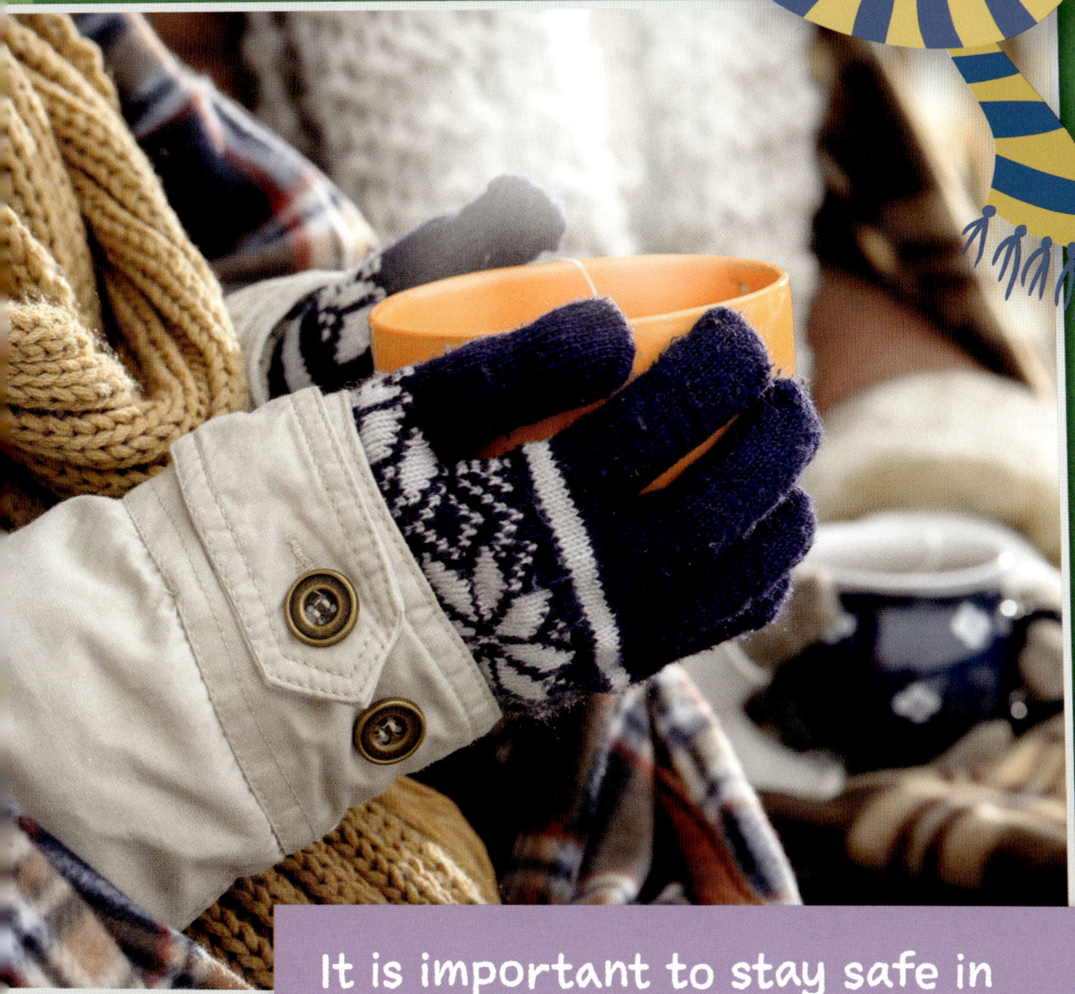

It is important to stay safe in cold weather. Take breaks inside. Drink something hot to warm up.

Be extra careful around roads. Snow can make it hard to see. Ice can make roads slippery to cross.

CHILLY DAYS

Cold days can be exciting. There are lots of great activities to do in cold weather.

Sledding and building snow forts make chilly days fun. Throw on your winter clothes, and enjoy the cold weather!

GLOSSARY

crystals solid objects that are shaped into regular patterns

hypothermia when the body's temperature becomes dangerously low

muscles parts of the body that help you move

shiver to shake or tremble

tilted leaning to one side

INDEX